‘Many younger Australians no longer feel that hard work brings a better life. In this timely book, Kells reveals the deeper, actual reasons Australia is no longer a land of economic opportunity.’

Thomas Walker, CEO, Think Forward

‘The thrust of this excellent work is that the process and consequences of the generation of money have been widely misunderstood by regulatory and government bodies, leading Australia unwittingly clinging to a “fragile prosperity”. Kells sets about offering practical solutions.’

David Merrett, Professor Emeritus, Faculty of Business and Economics, University of Melbourne

Stuart Kells is Enterprise Fellow at the Melbourne Institute, University of Melbourne, Adjunct Professor at La Trobe Business School, and has written extensively on economics and finance. He was formerly a member of the Program in Monetary and Financial Economics at the University of Melbourne and advised the Australian Bankers Association during the Wallis Inquiry into the Australian financial system. He won the Desmond Cleary Prize in Financial Economics and the KPMG Prize in Taxation Law at the University of Melbourne. He received the Potter Warburg Scholarship in Economics and Finance and the National Australia Bank Scholarship in Economics. He has twice won the Ashurst Business Literature Prize.

Public Matters

The Public Matters series comprises short books addressing pressing issues of public concern for Australians.

Other books in this series:

Curing Australia's Childcare Crisis: Quality, Universal Early Learning
Andrew Scott

FRAGILE PROSPERITY

AUSTRALIA'S GIGANTIC MONETARY GAMBLE

STUART KELLS

ANU PRESS

PUBLIC MATTERS

ANU PRESS

Published by ANU Press
The Australian National University
Canberra ACT 2600, Australia
Email: anupress@anu.edu.au

Available to download for free at press.anu.edu.au

The Australian National University acknowledges, celebrates and pays our respects to the Ngunnawal and Ngambri people of the Canberra region and to all First Nations Australians on whose traditional lands we meet and work, and whose cultures are among the oldest continuing cultures in human history.

ISBN (paperback): 9781760467425
ISBN (online): 9781760467418

DOI: 10.22459/FP.2026

Cover design and layout by ANU Press

Table of contents

Acknowledgements ix

Prelude
The colourful life of John Law 1

Part I
Challenging the monetary orthodoxy 9

Part II
Some possible implications 37

Part III
Conclusion 55

Postscript
Australia's final step in bank deregulation took place just last year 69

Appendix: Figures 71

References 75

Acknowledgements

This book is based on speeches delivered in 2025 to the Christopher Wren Society at the Windsor Hotel, Melbourne, and the Numismatic Association of Australia biennial conference at the Melbourne Law School, University of Melbourne.

The author is grateful to Ian Shepherd, John Creedy, Nathan Hollier and David Merrett, and to several reviewers for comments on an earlier version of the manuscript.

Prelude

The colourful life of John Law

Often referred to as the father of modern finance and modern money, John Law was the first 'finance bro' and the first rockstar economist. A prototype Elon Musk, he was the world's richest private citizen in his day and was appointed to a powerful role in the government of pre-revolutionary France.

Law was born in Cramond near Edinburgh in 1671. His family tree included clergymen and goldsmiths; his father came from the latter side of the tree.

Though John displayed an early talent with numbers, he never went to university. Instead, at age 14, he left school and went to work in his father's business.

Just three years later his father died. Law's apprenticeship was cut short and he moved to London where – thanks to his late father's money – he became a dandy and a gambler.

Initially he lost money at the gaming tables, but he had better luck in affairs of the heart. Tall, handsome and fashionably dressed, he had several love interests, including a possible entanglement with the Countess of Orkney, reputedly the King's mistress.

When Law was 23, his life took a drastic turn. Another dandy, Edward 'Beau' Wilson, challenged him to a duel. The precise reason is unknown. It may have been about the Countess or about Law's relationship with another woman, a Mrs Lawrence.

The combatants met at Bloomsbury Square. Wilson drew his sword first but Law promptly ran him through. It was a bloody encounter. Law was found guilty of murder.

Law petitioned strongly for release or for an alternative judgement of manslaughter. But Wilson's family fought hard to maintain the original conviction.

Facing the gallows or worse (such as being 'broken on the wheel'), Law escaped to the Continent, likely with the help of senior English officials, some of whom may have been bribed.

Over the span of a decade he lived in Amsterdam and Paris, and he visited other major European centres of finance, deepening his knowledge of economics and money.

In 1704 he returned to Scotland, which at the time was beyond the reach of English justice. He continued to work on economic matters and wrote an influential work that set out his views on how to improve the Scottish economy by increasing the money supply with paper money.[1]

Law saw major shortcomings in having a currency based on precious metals such as gold or silver, though this idea had a lot of supporters and several precedents. Most importantly, he said, the supply of those metals was arbitrary. Unexpected

1 Law (1705).

discoveries of gold or silver massively increased their availability, causing their value to drop. 'Silver was liable to a change in its value,' Law wrote, 'from any change in its quantity'.[2]

When people suddenly had more silver in their pockets and their vaults, the prices of everyday goods and services went up. The result was economy-wide inflation. Spain's New World possessions provided a spectacular example.

First discovered in 1545, the famous Cerro Rico ('rich mountain' or 'rich hill') near Potosí in Bolivia was a mountain of solid silver ore. Between 1556 and 1783 it yielded 45,000 tons of pure silver – and the result was inflation that spread from Spain right across Europe.

Law believed that over the long run, due to similar discoveries, the value of gold and silver would fall, making them unsuitable as the basis for a currency. A paper currency tied to gold or silver had other shortcomings, too, including the already widespread use of gold and silver in coinage and the long track record of kings devaluing and expropriating gold and silver currency by fiat.

Law proposed instead that the new paper money should be backed by land, so that the total value of the notes would equal the total value of a given amount of land.

2 ibid.

That fixed quantity, Law reasoned, would put a hard limit on money creation. Land values, moreover, would be stable, gently increasing over time as innovations in agriculture made land more productive.[3] And unlike a gold-based or silver-based paper currency, a land-based paper currency would unambiguously augment the existing stock of money. Hence, Law's proposal for a 'land bank' to manage the issuance of land-based loans and currency.

(Subsequent groups and authors have advocated versions of land banks, including the nineteenth-century authors of a submission to the wonderfully named 'Select Committee on Monetary Confusion' in the New South Wales parliament. The submission proposed 'a "Land Board" that would issue notes against real estate. The notes were to be legal tender, though not convertible into gold. The Legislative Council endorsed the proposal but [NSW] Governor Gipps refused to give it his assent'.[4])

Drawing on his experience in his father's business, Law also examined the emergence of the first commercial banks in Europe:

3 O'Brien (2007) on Law's 'Essay on a land bank':

> Law considered land to be a better basis for [currency] issue than silver, contrasting the rising long-run value of land with the falling long-run value of silver. He believed that this was due to agricultural improvements yielding greater output, as well as the fixity in supply. (p.47)

4 Gollan (1968), p.15.

> Banks have long been used in Italy, but as I'm informed, the invention of them was owing to Swedeland [Sweden]. Their money was copper, which was inconvenient, by reason of its weight and bulk; to remedy this inconveniency, a bank was set up where the money might be pledged, and credit given to the value, which passed in payments, and facilitated trade … Banks, where the money is pledged equal to the credit given, are sure [that is, safe]; for, though demands are made of the whole, the bank does not fail in payment.[5]

Law regularly likened banks to goldsmiths, and he saw bank lending as anchored in the quantity of deposits. The transformation of deposits into loans required some deft footwork to match assets (loans) and liabilities (deposits) of different maturities.

Deft footwork was also required to make sure the bank always had enough deposits in reserve. Taking the Bank of Amsterdam as an example, he described the phenomenon that was later called 'fractional reserve banking': a bank could lend out pledged deposits provided it maintained an adequate reserve for covering withdrawals. The danger here, as he explains, is a 'run' on deposits:

5 Law (1705).

> Yet if the whole demands were made, or demands greater than the remaining money, they could not all be satisfied, till the bank had called in what sums were lent.[6]

Meanwhile, the 1706 Act brought about the political union of England and Scotland, which was due to take effect from 1707. The union spelled great danger for Law, who was still officially on the run and wanted for murder. Before the Act took effect, he again escaped to the Continent, where his fortunes took another dramatic turn.

Thanks possibly to a meeting at a Parisian gaming table, Law befriended the libertine Duc d'Orléans, nephew of France's King Louis XIV. Orléans had considerable power in the French court, as the King was elderly and the heir to the throne was a child. Following the King's death, Orléans would serve as Regent from 1715 to 1723.

Law pressed Orléans to adopt his economic ideas and, after a series of false starts, the Scotsman was appointed Comptroller-General of Finances in the French government, a senior post that gave him the perfect opportunity to put his ideas into practice.

Law established a bank (the Banque Générale, subsequently renamed the Banque Royale) and he acquired a trading company that held France's commercial interests in the colony of Louisiana, whose principal settlement was named New Orleans

6 ibid.

in honour of the Duc. The company's interests encompassed a vast slice of the North American continent, extending upward from the Gulf of Mexico and into modern-day Canada. Other French overseas interests were also consolidated into the new enterprise, well known as the Mississippi Company.

Law's bank and company became testbeds for several unprecedented financial experiments that expanded the money supply, in turn feeding demand for shares in the Mississippi Company. The market price of those shares surged from 500 livres to 10,000 livres by December 1719. France buzzed with a widespread feeling of newfound wealth. Rents and property prices soared and people rushed to buy luxury goods. Law's experiment caused a massive tilt in investment and economic activity, reshaping the whole French economy.

The effects were profound, but temporary. The model and theories of an avid gambler turned out to be a house of cards.

The financial experiments sparked inflation – between July 1719 and December 1720 the price of goods doubled.

In the final months of 1720, the value of the Mississippi Company shares collapsed, and there was a run on Law's bank. His experiments and reputation came crashing down. To France, Law had brought only fragile and fleeting prosperity.

Forced to leave the country in haste and disguise, he survived for a time on his skills at the gaming tables but ultimately died in poverty in Venice in 1729.

Part I

Challenging the monetary orthodoxy

Money.

You don't need me to tell you how important it is. But for something so all-pervading, few people know how it actually works.

This would not matter except that widespread misunderstandings and false intuitions about money have powerful effects. In government, banking, journalism and academia, these misconceptions affect how people think, what they write and what they do.

I know this from direct experience in all these fields.

The modern monetary model is a muddle.

How did we get here?

Jes Black (2021) has done some excellent analysis and sleuthing to trace the problem back to incorrect textbook descriptions of bank credit creation. Particularly at fault was the influential 1985 volume *Economics* by Paul Samuelson and William Nordhaus.

Black is right to call out the wrongheaded textbooks of the 1980s, however (as he acknowledges), the monetary muddle demonstrably predates those publications. Early in the 1970s, for example, the breakdown of the international gold standard (as part of the Bretton Woods framework) changed the monetary system in fundamental ways with which many are still grappling.

And the muddle goes back much further than that – in fact, all the way back to John Law and his writings at the start of the eighteenth century.

In several ways, he was ground zero for our monetary muddle. To understand this, let's walk briefly through a picture of the current monetary orthodoxy.[1]

For many people with an active interest in the workings of the financial system, the following elements of an orthodox picture will be very familiar:

- Money circulates through the economy as an official, durable, tradable unit. These units are what we talk about when we speak, for example, of 'the Australian dollar', 'the Pound' or 'the US dollar'.
- Governments collect much of this money, holding it (figuratively in 'coffers') and then using it as the basis for government spending and investment.
- If governments spend more than they receive in taxation (in other words, if they are in deficit), this injects additional money into the economy, equal to the difference between the tax revenue and the spending.
- When people deposit money into bank accounts, the receiving banks use a large proportion of that money as the basis for loans, by 'lending out' the deposits. This is

1 In this discussion, I'll ignore coins and banknotes, which are only a very small proportion of the money supply today and are shrinking in importance.

the origin of the concept of a loan multiplier or credit multiplier, which explains how lending leads to deposits and further lending, thereby multiplying credit across the economy. It is also behind the idea that banks 'intermediate' between depositors and borrowers.

- A proportion of bank deposits is kept aside as reserves, as a safety margin for banks to cover transfers and withdrawals; hence the concept of fractional reserve banking.
- Central banks can influence the supply of money in the economy directly by altering the quantity of reserves in the financial system. This is why these reserves are referred to as 'base money'. When central banks increase the quantity of reserves in the banking system, we have 'quantitative easing'.
- Reserves held on deposit by private banks with the central bank are liabilities of the central bank, just as ordinary bank deposits are liabilities of commercial banks.
- Inflation – a sustained increase in the general price level – can be caused by multiple factors, including an excess of aggregate demand, government spending exceeding tax revenue, money creation by the central bank, and cost-push factors such as commodity price spikes (commonly caused by natural disasters or by wars) or substantial wage demands from workers.
- The best way for central banks to keep inflation at a reasonable level is through the active use of official interest rates to keep a lid on overall economic activity (a model of inflation targeting by central banks first formulated in New

Zealand at the end of the 1980s). Ideally, the fiscal policy stance (i.e. the size of the government budget surplus or deficit) will complement the monetary policy stance, so that fiscal and monetary policy as a whole constrain the economy in a way that keeps inflation under control.

You will find most of these nine propositions in the financial press every day, as well as on central bank websites, in economics and finance textbooks, and in government reports and policy statements.

However, these nine propositional elements of our accepted financial-system reality are all false, not just in a narrow technical sense, but in fundamental ways.

This is a big claim which, to be sustained, must be shown to be based on clearly identifiable monetary system misunderstandings, errors and falsehoods.

We need to set these out carefully, along with their implications. I will do this with a focus on Australia, which is doubly useful as a case study. First, Australia's monetary system is similar to those of equally advanced economies. Most of the findings about Australia are just as relevant to the US, the UK and many other countries. Second, features of Australia's policy settings and asset markets make the example of this nation especially illuminating. Australia pursued financial deregulation to a greater extent than most other countries, including even the US; and in recent decades Australia has experienced an exceptionally high rate of price growth in a single asset type, namely residential property.

John Law's life and work, as sketched in the Prelude, help explain why the intuitive orthodoxy of money and banking needs to be rethought.

Thanks to Law, the concept of fractional reserve banking is central to how finance is taught, and it is often invoked by commercial and central banks to explain how banking works.

Yet even in Law's day, the concept was an anachronism when applied to the first true modern banks, and it is even more of a myth now.

Law thought of banks as like goldsmiths – and there's a good reason for that. He grew up in a goldsmith's shop, at a time when the very first modern banks were appearing in Europe, many of them having begun as goldsmiths.

Fractional reserve banking was an accurate description of Law's father's business: some gold would be lent out, but a fraction would be retained to cover withdrawals and other instructions. Deposits, loans and reserves were all the same gold.

But the operation of banks is quite different. Banks do not gather up deposits and turn them into loans by 'lending them out'. Unlike goldsmiths, banks can create deposits at the stroke of a pen. This is why bank money is sometimes referred to as 'fountain pen money'.[2]

The loan funds that are created in this way are created costlessly. Let's hear that again: For banks, the direct marginal cash cost of creating new money for lending is zero.

The 2014 Bank of England paper 'Money creation in the modern economy' described contemporary bank money and how it is created through lending:

> In the modern economy, most money takes the form of bank deposits. But how those bank deposits are created is often misunderstood: the principal way is through commercial banks making loans. Whenever a bank makes a loan, it simultaneously creates a matching deposit in the borrower's bank account, thereby creating new money.

2 In a world in which bank deposits can be created by the stroke of a pen, banks do not compete for deposits; they compete for loan-creation opportunities.

> The reality of how money is created today differs from the description found in some economics textbooks: rather than banks receiving deposits when households save and then lending them out, bank lending creates deposits [that is, money in the economy directly].[3]

To summarise, in creating money through lending, banks do not transform deposits into loans, and they do not intermediate between depositors and borrowers. The two sides of banks' balance sheets are not intermingled.

The concepts of intermediation and of a 'lending multiplier' or 'credit multiplier' are based on misunderstandings of what banks do and how the financial system works.

Let's look at some of the other elements of the monetary orthodoxy and why they, too, are wrong.

3 McLeay et al. (2014), p.1. Also see Werner (2014), pp.1–19, Kells (2024a).

Taxation is not about governments collecting money to spend, but about removing liquidity from the economy

When the Australian government spends, it does so by creating new deposit balances in the private banking system. These augment the money supply. And when the government 'collects' taxes, it erases the balances that were used to pay the taxes; this erasure reduces the money supply.

The idea of federal tax payments being collected into 'coffers' is a widespread myth. Governments cannot hold bank money outside the banking system; bank money only exists if it is in a bank account.[4] Instead, taxation is a means to take liquidity out of the economy by destroying a quantum of bank money.[5]

The government also destroys money by borrowing through the sale of bonds to 'non-banks' (such as you and me). Taxation erases money permanently and involuntarily,

4 Even when governments and central banks create money, they do so through the private banking system. Physical currency is a partial exception here, insofar as it is created outside the commercial banking system; but it enters circulation through that system. So-called cryptocurrencies issued by non-bank, non-government actors are another partial exception, but in many respects they lack the properties of money.

5 As I will explain later in this book, bank money is contractual and ledger-based. A positive balance in a bank account is not a record of some form of durable, unitised money held somewhere for the account holder, and corresponding to the balance.

whereas government borrowing erases money temporarily and voluntarily. It is temporary because, at a later date, money is created to pay interest and the value of the loan.[6]

The federal government does not increase the money supply, even when the government budget is in deficit

The federal government operates under a self-imposed fiscal discipline such that the main account for managing the government's incoming and outgoing funds – the Official Public Account (OPA), held with the Reserve Bank – cannot have a negative balance.[7]

If proposed government spending exceeds taxation, the government must borrow from capital markets to maintain the positive account balance.[8] The money destroyed through taxation and (from non-banks) government borrowing always offsets the amount of bank money created through government spending.

6 Such as the face value of a bond.

7 The OPA is the Australian equivalent of the US government's Treasury General Account (TGA). The OPA balance convention is a strong operational practice, though not an absolute legal barrier to payment execution if Parliament has provided authority.

8 In May 2025, the Australian government's gross debt was approximately $1 trillion, and in net terms (after taking into account the government's financial assets), less than $600 billion. As noted, this does not represent net money creation.

Hence, there is no net creation of bank money by the Australian federal government.[9] This is the case for all forms of government spending (including grant provision) and government lending. And it is the case regardless of whether the budget is in surplus or deficit.

This reality is in contrast to a widely held and often repeated view that government spending and deficits are primary sources of inflation in the economy. (A recent example: in response to questions from a parliamentary committee on 6 February 2026, Reserve Bank Governor Michele Bullock stated government spending was contributing to high inflation in Australia.)[10] That view is wholly untrue and runs counter to how public finance works.

9 In referring to the Australian federal government, I am speaking of the 'non-consolidated' government: in other words, the government without the central bank.
10 Standing Committee on Economics (2026).

Bank lending is by far the main source of new money creation in the Australian economy: in effect, we have privatised our currency and the process of money creation

In principle, in countries like Australia that are 'monetarily sovereign' (i.e. they have their own currency), new money can come from three potential sources: the national government, the central bank and private banks.[11]

But as I've noted, the federal government – due to a self-imposed discipline – does not create new money.

The Reserve Bank of Australia (RBA) does create net new money from time to time, though only on a modest scale. (Strictly speaking, by purchasing securities such as government bonds, the RBA causes the private banking system to create this new money.[12] If the RBA purchases the securities from banks, there is no net change in the money supply, only changes in

11 For an open economy with a floating exchange rate, financial flows from international trade and investment do not affect the money supply, as any surplus or deficit on the current account – for international trade in goods and services – is exactly offset by a corresponding deficit or surplus on the capital account, with the exchange rate adjusting to maintain this balance.

12 The RBA purchases securities from non-banks via exchange settlement account holders. Thus, the money created by this process is bank money, but triggered by the RBA's actions.

holdings of reserves and securities; but when the RBA buys them from non-banks, this adds money into the financial system by causing commercial banks to create money.)

The RBA does not publish data on its direct impact on the money supply, but that impact is only a small proportion of total money creation in Australia. We know this because we can see the relationship between bank lending and total money supply growth. The RBA does not use direct money creation as a principal tool of monetary policy.

This leaves the commercial banks. The great majority of money is created by these banks in giant, silent mints that produce masses of money at the stroke of electronic pens. In Australia, as in many other countries, therefore, the national system of money creation is for the most part privately owned and orchestrated.

When Canadian–American economist and author John Kenneth Galbraith first learnt of how bank money was created, he was shocked: 'the process by which banks create money is so simple that the mind is repelled. Where something so important is involved, a deeper mystery seems only decent.'[13]

In Australia the 'money power' given to private banks was the subject of intense debate in the nineteenth century. An economic slump from 1841 to 1843 saw a spike in insolvencies and commercial bank failures, leading to pressure

13 Galbraith (2017).

for currency reform and the creation of a publicly owned bank. That New South Wales parliamentary committee – the 'Select Committee on Monetary Confusion' mentioned in the Prelude – was established to consider monetary reform options. Influential politician William Charles Wentworth argued the money power ought to rest with the state: 'the power of issuing circulating medium … had been imperceptibly taken away from the hands of Government, to which it alone could be safely entrusted'.[14]

Though bank money is far and away the most important form of money in the economy, its nature is still widely misunderstood

Putting aside coins and notes, which today are almost irrelevant, we do not have a system of official, durable, unitised currency that circulates through the economy.

Instead, we have a ledger-based system of contractual, written-down credit. The 'movement' of money between two banks involves reducing a ledger balance in the paying bank and increasing it in the receiving bank. Sitting behind the ledger balance, there are no units or tokens. The balance is all there is.

14 Gollan (1968), p.15.

That balance is 'digital' only insofar as the ledgers and associated payment systems are computerised. And it is 'official' only indirectly, insofar as banks and the financial systems are regulated by government. Because bank money is contractual and ledger-based, and neither unitised nor durable, it is not tradable.[15]

Aside from notes and coins, 'the Australian dollar', 'the Pound' and 'the US dollar' exist only in an abstract sense, as does the 'money market' in the sense of a market in ordinary bank money.[16]

The distinctive feature of modern banking is a two-tier system of deposits and reserves

This two-tier system is what differentiates banks from goldsmiths.

With goldsmiths, as noted, deposits are gold, and so are reserves. With banks, in contrast, the deposits are lower-quality, ledger-based and pen-created IOUs, whereas the reserves are of a higher quality than deposits, and they are used to settle inter-bank payments.

15 Moves are afoot in some parts of the world to create tradable tokens that are backed by bank account funds.

16 With the term 'money market', I am referring here specifically to trading in bank money. Other forms of 'money markets' exist, including markets for securities that provide short-term credit. Also, I note again that there are innovations underway that seek to tokenise and securitise bank money.

The lower-quality, ledger-based IOUs depend on the creditworthiness of the bank at which the deposits are held. The higher-quality reserves (which may be in the form of gold, government-issued banknotes or, in more recent times, central bank balances) do not.[17]

For banks, therefore, fractional reserve banking is a misnomer because reserves are not a subset of deposits. This mode of banking should perhaps instead be called 'proportional reserve banking'.

There is far from a one-to-one correspondence between bank deposits and reserves. Much of the daily work of banking does not involve reserves at all. For example, payments and transfers between accounts within an individual bank are effected simply through ledger entries; and many inter-bank transfers and payments are offset by payments and transfers in the opposite direction, and so they are 'netted', again not requiring the involvement of reserves.

17 Reserves are also used to settle inter-country payments.

Financial deregulation in Australia removed direct limits on money creation by banks

In 1979, the government of Prime Minister Malcolm Fraser established the Campbell Committee of Inquiry into the Australian financial system. The committee's 1981 final report to Treasurer John Howard recommended accelerating the process of Australian financial system deregulation that had begun in the 1960s.[18]

Prior to that program, there were strict and multifaceted controls on bank lending and, therefore, private money creation in Australia. The controls related to the size of bank loans, the interest rates that could be charged, and the purposes and types of lending, such as for business loans and housing construction.

Why were the controls removed?

A large part of the rationale for deregulation was to restore the market share of banks, which had been losing out to building societies, life insurance companies and other types of institutions in the lending market.

The hope was that banks, freed from undue regulation, would be better able to compete with other types of financial institutions, and would become major sources of productive credit, thereby spurring economic growth and national development.

18 Campbell Committee of Inquiry (1981).

Deregulation did indeed accelerate. In June 1982, for example, the government largely removed quantitative lending controls, which had hitherto, among other things, placed ceilings on the interest rates that could be charged to borrowers.[19]

In May 1985, Reserve Bank Governor RA Johnston was able to state,

> We now have a virtually fully deregulated financial system – at least in the monetary management sense. Indeed, we have deregulated the financial system as far and as fast as any country.[20]

In removing restrictions on lending in particular, Australia went further than nearly all the other advanced economies. The United States, for example, retained a variety of rules that regulated mortgage size and banking practices, including through the roles played by 'Fannie Mae' and 'Freddie Mac'[21] in providing liquidity, stability and affordability.

---

19 An exception: a cap of 13.5 per cent applied to pre-existing housing loans until 1986.

20 Johnston (1985).

21 Fannie Mae (Federal National Mortgage Association) and Freddie Mac (Federal Home Loan Mortgage Corporation) are shorthand names for two government-sponsored enterprises that aim to stabilise the US housing market by buying mortgages from lenders, providing liquidity for new loans and selling mortgage-backed securities to investors.

The result of financial deregulation in Australia was a big shift from non-money-creating lenders to money-creating lenders

As bank lending is the primary mechanism of money creation, the removal of limits on lending meant the removal of an important set of limits on money creation.

With financial deregulation, therefore, Australia had embarked on a huge monetary experiment, on a scale that exceeded Law's experiment in eighteenth-century France.

Though the banks had been given a new and less fettered currency power, few if any people thought of this, and the level of debate about the impact of deregulation on money creation was remarkably small.

From an historical perspective, money creation through mortgage lending is somewhat novel in Australia. Prior to deregulation, a high proportion of mortgages were issued by life insurers and building societies, and even by high-wealth individuals and solicitors' trust funds.[22]

22 Merrett (2000), pp.237–38.

The mortgages issued by those institutions and individuals typically involved using money that already existed – such as funds already held in the bank, or funds raised by selling securities or insurance – and therefore did not create new money.[23]

By dramatically increasing the market share of banks, financial deregulation significantly altered the extent to which lending involved new money creation.

The end of the Bretton Woods system transformed the role of central banks and reserves

Endorsed by the Allied powers in 1944 and put into force in 1945, the Bretton Woods framework linked Western countries' currencies to the gold-backed US dollar. That system continued until the early 1970s when it broke down under the strain of inflation and a shifting global financial system.

The immediate cause occurred during Richard Nixon's presidency. Previous US governments had been reluctant to raise taxes to pay for the war in Vietnam. Fearing the US dollar

23 Australia's big banks are sometimes likened to giant building societies because they have retreated from business lending and now mainly lend for real estate purchases. But there are important differences between banks and building societies. As noted, banks are differently owned, governed and regulated.

was overvalued, foreign central banks sought to redeem their extensive dollar holdings for gold. Nixon ordered Treasury Secretary John Connally to suspend the convertibility of the dollar into gold.

The US and other advanced economies switched to a pure 'fiat' system that settled foreign exchange transactions in central bank balances. Gold was no longer the international reserve currency.

This was a very significant change, with implications that are still being felt. One key consequence: the settlement medium could now be created at no direct cost, just like bank deposits and very much unlike gold, which is of limited supply and has a high commodity value.

The world is still grappling with this new reality, as revealed in several important ways I will return to discuss.

Central bank reserves are clearing and settlement units: they do not determine the quantity of private bank lending

As noted above, the RBA causes private banks to create net new money from time to time, on a modest scale, by purchasing securities from non-banks.

In addition to such instances of bank deposit creation, the RBA regularly injects reserves into the system, in the form of exchange settlement account funds or ESAs – these are our form of reserves under the post–Bretton Woods system.[24]

ESAs are counted as an important part of 'base money' (also known as M0 and 'high-powered money'), but they are not properly money because, among other things, non-banks cannot hold or use them; they are not directly part of the purchasing economy.

As I noted in my description of the monetary orthodoxy, reserves are widely regarded as the foundation for money creation on the grounds that they are seen as determining the level of commercial bank lending.

On that basis, according to a longstanding argument, central banks can control money creation in the economy by controlling the quantum of reserves available to the banking system.

For several reasons, these popular ideas, associated with George Warde Norman, Robert Torrens and Lord Overstone (Samuel Jones Loyd), among many others, are untrue.[25]

24 The RBA injects reserves into the financial system when it purchases securities and when net government spending is positive. Later in the book I will explore how ESAs are accounted for.

25 See, for example, Norman (1841), Torrens (1812) and Loyd (1858).

In ordinary circumstances, the quantity of reserves neither determines nor limits the level of money creation by commercial banks. The balance sheets of commercial and central banks have been substantively decoupled. As the Bank of England noted in 2014, 'In normal times, the central bank does not fix the amount of money in circulation, nor is central bank money "multiplied up" into more loans and deposits'.[26]

The relationship between reserves and loan creation is not straightforward.

As noted, a significant proportion of bank money transfers and payments do not involve reserves; these payments and transfers occur within a bank. The quantum of reserves needed for inter-bank payments, moreover, is affected by practices such as 'netting', which means equal but offsetting payments between banks cancel each other out, requiring settlement only of the net amount.[27] In Australia, as the biggest banks have grown together, the flow of inter-bank payments has become more predictable, and the quantum of reserves required for inter-bank settlement has fallen in proportional terms.[28]

---

26 McLeay et al. (2014), p.1. And as the Federal Reserve Bank of St Louis noted in 2018: 'While the Fed's control over the size of the monetary base is complete, its control over the money supply is not' (FRB St Louis, 2018).

27 Netting has been an important feature of banking and finance since at least the seventeenth century.

28 Keynes made a similar point in his 1930 *A Treatise on Money*. In principle, he wrote, there was 'no limit to the amount of bank money which the banks [could] safely create provided that they move[d] forward in step'. If all banks expanded lending at the same pace, they could expand the money supply without running short of reserves.

Loan creation by any major bank occurs alongside a reliable inflow of deposits into that bank, with those deposits having been created by that same bank's earlier loan creation and by loan creation in other banks. Even when bank money is used to buy equities or is transferred to superannuation accounts, it goes directly into bank accounts. (To reiterate, bank money only exists if it is in a bank account.) Inflowing deposits (in net terms) bring reserves with them.

In other respects, too, reserves are easy to come by in our monetary system. Banks can obtain them from the 'repurchase agreement market' (known as the 'repo market'), such as in exchange for government bonds. (The repo market provides secured, short-term funding for financial institutions.)

As a matter of policy, the RBA is generous with reserves, which, as noted, are created costlessly, and which banks are compensated for holding, as the RBA pays interest to banks on ESA funds.

During the Covid pandemic, the RBA moved to a system of 'abundant' reserves. The ESA holdings of Australian banks with the RBA jumped from less than $100 billion to more than $400 billion. Since that time, the holdings have fallen back but the RBA's policy is still to have 'ample' reserves.

A further reason why ESAs do not limit money creation is that the RBA does not have a complete monopoly on inter-bank settlement units. Banks can still settle payments among themselves with other assets such as notes and coins, gold bullion and claims to gold; and more importantly, they can defer settlement through the provision of interbank credit.

For these and other reasons, a longstanding debate about whether the quantum of reserves determines the quantum of commercial bank lending has now been resolved. It does not, and nor does it determine interest rates or exchange rates.[29]

Rather than as a form of money, central bank reserves are better thought of as a regulatory artefact: 'clearing and settlement units' which run alongside inter-bank and international transactions in bank money, giving an official stamp to those transactions.

Private bank lending, together with the velocity of money, determines the rate of inflation in Australia

The 'quantity theory of money' is properly not a theory but an accounting tautology, MV=PT.

29 The RBA pays interest on commercial banks' ESA holdings; this interest rate does affect market interest rates. I am distinguishing here between the quantum of reserves and the rate of interest paid on the reserves.

Stated in words, this equation means the money stock (M) multiplied by the velocity of money (how quickly the money circulates, V) corresponds to nominal aggregate expenditure in the economy, measured as the price level multiplied by the number of transactions (PT).

An alternative way to express the equation is MV=PY: the money stock multiplied by the velocity corresponds to the nominal value of national income, expressed as the product of prices and real income (PY).

The quantity 'theory', or condition, means growth in the general price level depends on changes in the money supply and the velocity of money.

As the velocity of money has fallen consistently in Australia since the 1990s (see Appendix Figure 3: Quantity theory of money), all inflation since that time was caused by money supply growth. And as nearly all money supply growth was via bank lending, nearly all inflation in Australia over the past three decades has been caused by bank lending.[30] This has been true year after year, even during the height of the Covid pandemic, when the RBA was pumping reserves into the financial system.

Other factors familiarly cited as causes of inflation – such as aggregate demand, input cost increases, market concentration, industrial power, agricultural shortages and external shocks – cannot increase inflation without a corresponding increase in

30 This is borne out in the data on inflation and lending, even from the 1970s.

the money supply. Otherwise, there is insufficient money to give economic expression to the high demand or the rising costs, meaning they cannot occur. In order to purchase a given level of nominal output, there must be sufficient money in the hands of people and institutions to make the purchase.

The factors other than the quantum and velocity of money – such as demand, costs and industrial power – merely determine the *composition* or incidence of a given level of inflation, with that level determined by the money supply and its velocity.

Part II

Some possible implications

This is all very interesting, you might say, but what does it mean for the real economy and everyday life?

Let's follow some trains of thought about how Australia's monetary architecture is likely having significant real effects.

One of these trains of thought considers money creation and the housing market. It begins with John Law's land bank proposal and the idea of basing money creation on land.

Law had imagined that property-based currency issuance would be both financially reliable and economically neutral, with little impact on relative prices. But as economist Denis O'Brien and others have observed, the fundamental premise – that the value of land was independent of the money supply – was mistaken.

When land is used as the foundation for money creation, the value of the land is not independent of the money thus created. Instead, such property-based money creation has the unintended consequence of driving up property values, which in turn are the basis for a higher quantum of currency issuance.[1] And so the cycle continues, disconnecting land from its true value based on its productive use.

---

1 O'Brien (2007) on Law:

His view [of land as a sound basis for currency issuance] involved a basic fallacy, since it made the value of land independent of the money supply, which it clearly was not, as the fiasco of the Assignats in revolutionary France was to demonstrate conclusively. (p.47)

Law's prescription of a land-based currency is highly relevant to Australia. The largest share of money creation in our economic system takes place through private bank lending for real estate. For all intents and purposes, we have adopted a version of Law's model of land-based currency issuance.

As of May 2025, the total outstanding mortgage debt owed to private banks by investors and owner–occupiers in Australia was $2.4 trillion. This figure is the net quantum of money created by private banks through mortgage lending. It is much larger than the quantum of money created by the Australian government (which, as a result of the self-imposed fiscal accounting constraint, is nil) and by the Reserve Bank (which, as noted, creates a modest amount of net new money from time to time).

Since deregulation (and congruent with deregulation's purpose), banks have gained a much larger share of the mortgage market. To a significant extent, this has been at the expense of other types of lending, as the profile of bank lending has tilted away from commercial loans. The ratio of home mortgages to commercial lending increased from 1.1 in the early 2000s to 1.9 today.[2] Also, a greater proportion of mortgage lending is now for investors acquiring multiple properties.[3]

---

2 One cause of this trend: large corporates no longer rely on banks to provide or 'syndicate' loans; the corporates can issue bonds directly, and they can tap other capital markets; see Kells (2024a).

3 See, for example, RBA (2017). Also see figures in the Appendix.

Australia's capital adequacy framework for banks is a locally modified version of the international Basel framework. Under this framework, banks must hold capital commensurate with the risks of the loans they write. The requirement to hold capital is greater for loans that are assessed as higher risk. Mortgage lending attracts the lowest risk weighting (relative to all other lending categories, including commercial property, small business lending, corporate lending and property development). This provides a strong, systemic incentive for the banks to emphasise mortgage lending.

Banks can advance as many property-based loans as they wish, subject only to (i) the capacity of borrowers, (ii) banks' assessment of the expected risk-adjusted profitability of their lending, and (iii) banks continually meeting their Basel capital adequacy requirements. Because of the nature of money creation by banks, there is a continuing supply of money for lending; and likewise, for a number of reasons, there is no shortage of borrowers.

To summarise: the great majority of money creation in the Australian economy occurs through debt-funded purchases of real estate, in particular existing real estate as opposed to new dwellings.[4] As a result of our current legal and institutional arrangements, this is the main way that new money is created in Australia.

4 The money is only created if the loan is made, and therefore if the property is purchased; and the property is only purchased if the borrower wins the auction, whichever format it takes.

Since 1988, the ratio of household debt to disposable income in Australia has risen from around 65 per cent to 180 per cent, and nearly all of that growth has been due to mortgage debt. House prices have increased at double the national inflation rate. Property prices have also grown much faster than incomes, and the growth has been remarkably consistent; it has continued despite financial crises, the Covid emergency and other calamities over the past four decades. The total value of residential properties in Australia (land and buildings) has reached the extraordinarily large figure of $11 trillion.[5]

Two generations of policy decisions have resulted in a circular engine of money creation through borrowing. The engine mostly involves changes of ownership of existing properties at higher and higher prices.[6] Systemic factors, such as taxation incentives and the presence of wealth effects from property ownership, help perpetuate this process.

Overall, Australia's national system of taxation and transfers – including negative gearing, favourable capital gains tax treatment and various direct subsidies such as home buyer grants – has favoured bank lending based on real estate. Also, rising property prices have a wealth effect, which is partly real and partly a perception, and which gives property owners a higher capacity and a greater willingness to borrow. Recent McKinsey

5 By way of comparison, the total value of non-residential land here is $1.5 trillion.

6 The cycle of increasing loan sizes is why loan-asset ratios are also not a limit on bank money creation.

research showed that, since 2008, the average net wealth of Australians had doubled, and as much as 70 per cent of that increase came from property values.[7]

Over the past four decades, Australians have spent a larger and larger share of their income on housing-related costs, including mortgage repayments. Housing costs as a share of income are well above historic benchmark levels. The proportion of income needed to meet mortgage repayments has risen from less than 25 per cent to more than 50 per cent. As Alan Kohler noted in his 2023 Quarterly Essay, *The Great Divide*, this is the most important factor in Australia's economy today. That same year, National Australia Bank Chief Executive Andrew Irvine said access to housing was Australia's 'biggest societal and policy challenge'.[8]

The ratcheting up of mortgage costs has been underway since the 1980s, gradually crowding out other spending. For individual households, the ratchet can continue until something breaks and the borrower must default. But even then, the banks are largely insulated because they have good security, and they do well in selling the property into a generally rising market (thanks in large part to the impact of the money creation process, which tends to support overall house

7 Bradley et al. (2025), p.1.
8 NAB (2025).

prices). They also have other financial and legal protections and, for the largest banks, the ultimate insurance of an effective taxpayer guarantee.

This train of thought probably goes a long way to explaining why Australia, the country with among the fewest restrictions on bank money issuance, has also had the largest increase in house prices of any country in the OECD.[9]

Seen in this light, the growth in Australian property prices may not be a free-market phenomenon or a national boon. Instead, it could merely be an artefact of monetary forcing caused by the system itself and the commercial banks' money-creation function. In that case, the effects of the property boom would be like John Law's impact on eighteenth-century France: fragile prosperity.

Another train of thought: Banks' profitability may be out of step with the risks they manage and the economic value they add.

9 Some countries, such as Canada and New Zealand, have gone down a similar path as Australia in removing lending restrictions, and they have experienced a similar pattern of property price growth.

I have described a cycle of monetary forcing in which bank lending drives up asset values, which are used as collateral for ever larger loans. This cycle is congruent with the observed size of the Australian banking sector and the profitability of individual Australian banks.

Banking is not directly productive. Financial services are 'intermediate products [that are] libations of oil on the machinery of industrial society – activities intended to eliminate friction in the productive system, not net contributions to ultimate consumption.'[10]

And yet banking is measured as a component of GDP, and it is taking up a larger and larger share of that measure of national output. Whether banking should be counted in GDP was, in the century before our current one, the subject of debate.

Between 1990 and 2024, the share of financial services in Australia's GDP rose from less than 6 per cent to more than 8 per cent. Other estimates put the share much higher than this. Over the same time period, the share of manufacturing in the economy approximately halved.

Speculative trading in existing real estate is also essentially unproductive and, when fed by disproportionate money supply growth, distorts the economy at the aggregate level.

10 Kuznets (1951), p.162.

The economic costs of unfettered money creation through mortgage lending are not borne by the big banks, which are now among the biggest and most profitable companies in Australia and indeed in the world. At the same time, the level of foreign ownership of the big banks is substantial, meaning a significant proportion of the banks' profits – more than a quarter – ends up overseas.

The list of Australia's eight largest companies includes five banks: the 'big four' plus Macquarie. One of the five banks is Australia's largest company, the Commonwealth Bank, originally founded as a public enterprise with an ethos of social benefit and the public good.

This phenomenon of high bank profitability in connection to unfettered bank money creation is analogous to the 'Cantillon Effect'.

In the eighteenth century, economist Richard Cantillon rightly conjectured that the source of new money in the economy mattered. The 'Cantillon Effect' describes how, when new money enters an economy, the first recipients are the ones who tend to benefit most from it and are able to claim the economic rents associated with it.

This effect is why the largest executive salaries are paid in the banking sector. As Alan Kohler showed in his book *It's Your Money* (2019), big banks were where Australian executive salaries really broke out, with the appointment of Bob Joss at Westpac. His remuneration package was seen as huge at the time, but today the private bank executives' packages are vastly larger.

There is a big disconnect between the banks' profits, the bankers' salaries and what those bankers actually do. Despite what John Law claimed, banks are quite easy to manage. They don't turn deposits into loans, nor do they intermediate between borrowers and lenders. Their assets and liabilities are neatly quarantined.

On the lending side, the crucial function of credit assessment has been commoditised and automated. The loans, moreover, are well backed by collateral. The rate of loan losses is very low (see Appendix Figure 4: Australian bank profits).

On the deposit side, the risks for banks are even smaller. The concept of a 'run on deposits' is a carryover from Law's anachronistic concept of fractional reserve banking. In order to function, banks do not need deposits per se; in fact, in and of themselves, deposits are for banks a costly nuisance.[11]

---

11 Deposits are useful insofar as the inflow of deposits from other banks also brings reserves, in net terms. They are also useful for commercial purposes, as part of banks' 'service offering'; and the receipt and management of deposits is often a condition of bank licences. But deposits qua deposits are liabilities for banks, and banks can function quite happily without them, provided the banks have sufficient reserves, which are costlessly created by the central bank.

The real risk from a run is that a bank will run out of reserves. But today, those reserves are in unlimited (and costless) supply from central banks, so the only real risk from a run is that the central bank does not move quickly enough to cover the deposit withdrawals with sufficient reserves. No bank should fail from a run under our present system.

Let's consider another line of thought, this time about how the money creation process, combined with central bank inflation targeting, could affect the wider economy.

In 2026, we have something that was not imagined in John Law's day: a central bank that pursues an inflation target.

Through an agreement with the federal government, as expressed in the Statement on the Conduct of Monetary Policy, the RBA is charged with using its powers to keep annual Australian CPI (consumer price index) inflation between 2 and 3 per cent.[12]

12 The inflation target benefits the private banks as it protects the real value of their loans. The monetary policy mechanism itself, moreover, delivers large and direct benefits to the banks. To constrain inflation, the RBA increases the rate of interest that is paid on bank reserves; and it green-lights increases in mortgage interest rates, allowing the banks to charge more for new and existing customers.

Bank lending has driven the great majority of money supply growth in Australia, and the resulting growth has been well above inflation: M3, a measure of the money supply that includes bank deposits, has grown on average by more than 8 per cent per annum since the early 1990s.

Given the relationship between money and inflation, why has this monetary growth not been manifested in reported inflation?

Returning to what is referred to as the quantity theory of money, if the velocity of money had remained constant, then inflation as a result of M3 growth would have exceeded 8 per cent annually on average, and in some years it would have been well over 10 per cent. But the velocity of money in Australia has fallen strongly and consistently, dropping by around 50 per cent since the early 1990s.

Velocity is a measure of spending frequency – and it is also an important indicator of economic vibrancy.

The collapse in velocity is striking. It suggests that the whole economy could be bearing an additional burden to offset the inflationary impact of the money-creating cycle. The collapse in velocity indicates that Australia has had three decades of belt tightening, deferred expenditure, and purchases of less liquid and less productive assets – primarily residential property.

This anti-inflation burden could manifest in the form of higher taxation, higher interest rates and a higher exchange rate. (Recall that taxation involves the destruction of purchasing power [almost entirely in the form of bank money] to help limit inflation. Bond issuance to fund higher budget deficits imposes costs on taxpayers due to the future financing burden. When the government borrows, moreover, this puts 'super credit-risk-free money' into the system [in the form of government securities], further heightening inequality because this money goes to, and is only useable by, sophisticated financial market participants. And finally, when the government increases taxes, these taxes are usually relatively regressive.)

It is a mathematical necessity that, for Australia to have 8 per cent annual money supply growth and 2.5 per cent annual inflation, everything else (i.e. the non-bank economy) must slow down – not just at the margin but to a very material extent.

This slowing, as revealed in the drop in the velocity of money, would be felt by households and individuals as a loss of financial headroom and economic opportunities.

The implications for the non-bank, non-mining parts of the economy could be very significant. Manufacturing in particular would be subject to a dual impact of the conventional Dutch disease from mining, with this one sector of the economy rapidly outpacing all others, plus a monetary Dutch disease of the form described here.

Declines in manufacturing are self-reinforcing. As Australia's manufacturing sector shrinks, we lose many of the supporting services and businesses, and our economy captures less and less of the value of tacit knowledge and 'learning by doing'. Instead, we end up paying for other countries' innovations.[13]

Across the economy as a whole, productive enterprises would lose out while the real estate and banking industries would benefit. Instead of manifesting as inflation, therefore, the over-issuance of property-based money would be seen in a gradual hollowing out and strangulation of the non-bank parts of the economy.

What are the implications for fiscal policy of a better understanding of money creation, inflation and taxation?

Borrowing to fund deficits has reached extraordinary levels around the world, most notably in the US. But the impetus to borrow arises from the self-imposed (and misguided) budget constraint mentioned earlier.[14]

---

13 Highlighting the importance of tacit knowledge in productivity and economic performance, US Federal Reserve of St Louis economist Yi Wen defined that knowledge as the practical know-how involved 'in the art of making things, in organizing practical matters, and in the way people produce, distribute, travel, communicate, and consume' (Wen [2015], p.109).

14 In a monetarily sovereign country, there is no need to borrow from capital markets to make up a budget deficit. This is a big subject, for another time.

More important than balancing the national budget is ensuring that total money creation – and therefore inflation – is kept at reasonable levels. Rather than a budget constraint, therefore, fiscal policy operates within an inflation constraint. This suggests a different understanding of Australia's total fiscal capacity.

In a meaningful sense, the true fiscal 'budget' for annual beneficial public expenditure at the national level is equal to taxation and government borrowing plus the level of annual money creation commensurate with the RBA's target rate of inflation.

In other words, annual money supply growth up to the target inflation rate represents a large and untapped source of funding for publicly beneficial investments. At the moment, Australians are probably wasting a great deal of Australia's total fiscal capacity. Specifically, much of the fiscal 'headroom' within the inflation constraint is being squandered on excessive lending for purchases of non-productive assets.

Let's look at one final set of implications arising from how we account for money at the aggregate level and model the financial system and the whole economy accordingly.

I have explained how central bank reserves should be thought of as functional, non-money units for clearing and settlement. The central bank can create any amount of these units (by 'fiat'), and it has no obligation to exchange them for any other type of asset, such as gold.

Current accounting of reserves, however, is a carryover from the pre-fiat era. By convention, reserves are conceived of as funds on deposit with the central bank, and they are accounted for as liabilities on the central bank's balance sheet.[15]

This convention can have significant consequences, and arguably perverse ones. A surge in reserve creation, for example, can leave a central bank with negative equity, even though the reserves are created costlessly by the central bank and give rise to no financial liabilities.

To maintain the convention of reserves as liabilities while avoiding negative equity, central banks must ensure they have commensurate assets on their balance sheet to offset the reserve 'liabilities'.

In addition to the potential mis-accounting of reserves, they are regularly and wrongly included in definitions of money.

15 Some central banks, including the RBA, have elected to pay interest to banks on their ESA holdings; this is arguably undesirable on several grounds. It is inconsistent, for example, with the ESAs' true nature and purpose as clearing and settlement units; and it causes a large transfer of wealth from taxpayers to private banks, outside (in Australia's case) the normal budgetary scrutiny of the national parliament.

These definitional issues become crucially important when central banks and other economic institutions use economic models to inform policy decisions.

Models that rely on the monetary orthodoxy and current monetary accounting are materially ill-conceived or, to be more precise, mis-specified: they are modelling the wrong phenomena in the wrong way.

Mis-specifications, then, arise from treating reserves as money, treating reserves as a liability of the central bank, failing to capture the two-tiered nature of the banking system, and incorrectly characterising the impact of the government's fiscal position on the money supply, inflation and economic activity. Including commercial banks in GDP figures is possibly another instance of mis-accounting that could lead to misleading modelling results.

The widespread reliance on economic models across the major economies means that incorrect data and assumptions within these can have very significant impacts. Further, incorrect expressions of concepts such as money, taxation and credit can intrude into contracts and legislation, potentially with similarly debilitating consequences.

Part III

Conclusion

Australia faces a conundrum in public policy and macroeconomic management

How are Australians going in 2026? Let's do a quick health check.

If you stand far enough away, things look OK.

Inflation, while high, has fallen back from its Covid-era spike. The unemployment rate is low, and GDP growth is rosy.

For a high proportion of households, however, the feeling is very different. Many people report being squeezed and struggling to get ahead, even with well-paying jobs.

The squeeze is most acute for people from younger generations, especially those who are trying to buy a home. But it cuts across all generations and all regions of Australia. The macroeconomic data confirm this mixed picture. The economy is growing, however, per capita income is falling, and inequality is rising.

For people who depend on public funding, the times are especially lean. 'Austerity' defines the era. But even in the private sector, economic conditions are distinctly uneven. A few industry sectors thrive while many others are under pressure.

We have not had a complete and compelling explanation for Australia's current economic performance – one that explains, for example, the sources and levels of money supply growth, the striking pace and resilience of Australian house price growth, the collapse in the velocity of money, and what that collapse reveals: the economic pressures faced by many households and by non-housing and non-mining sectors such as manufacturing.

Such an explanation may be derived, I am suggesting, from an analysis of Australia's giant experiment with modern money, more often referred to as the deregulation of the banking sector. That experiment gave private banks a near monopoly on money creation, and it removed most limits on the exercise of that monopoly.

The resulting currency-collateral-currency cycle affects the real economy in crucial ways. It causes excessive inflation, which elicits a monetary policy response; it affects relative prices of property and other assets, and of property and non-capital goods; and it affects the sectoral composition of the economy by favouring some sectors at the expense of others.

Economic distortion from money-forced property price growth is likely entrenching disadvantage and intergenerational inequality. It may be the principal cause of our intergenerational problem.

With our acute public austerity and imbalanced money creation, moreover, projects that promise strong economic, social and environmental benefits are not being funded.

The rewards reaped by commercial banks are a modern incarnation of the 'Cantillon Effect'. The organisations at the source of new money in the economy are the ones that receive the greatest benefits from the augmentation of the money supply.

The 2008 global financial crisis stemmed from the wholesale conversion of mortgages into securities, followed by risky bets on those securities. Instead of mortgage securitisation, Australia has pursued the unfettered creation of a mortgage-backed currency. This is unlikely to cause a financial crash; instead, its impact is playing out gradually, torpefyingly, and it could be causing the slow death of the non-bank economy.

Something terrible seems to have happened in Australia's economic stewardship, but are our policymakers talking about our national state of affairs in these terms?

Policymakers have focused on the wrong causes and used the wrong levers.

Facilitating the gaining of market share by money-creating banks at the expense of building societies and other non-money-creating lenders – without thinking through the implications of this for the financial system and the economy – was a foundational policy mistake.

The next mistake was to allow banks to prioritise residential-property-based lending. The Basel capital accord places a very low weighting on property-based lending. Adopted in Australia with minor modifications, the accord has been a big cause of why banks have emphasised mortgage lending in contrast to lending to productive businesses.

A compounding key error was the assumption that bank money creation would be systemically limited – either by the need to obtain deposits, or by active monetary policy levers. In actuality, the only limits on bank money creation were banks' commercial judgements and borrowers' appetites for loans. That appetite has been directly affected by the very process of bank lending driving up property prices.

As a result of unfettered bank money creation, average annual money supply growth has been more than three times the desired level. But, as I've noted, we have something John Law didn't have: a central bank with a rigorous inflation target.

Through the action of the RBA, in concert with government fiscal policy, Australia has kept inflation in check by suppressing other economic activity – as revealed by the collapse in money velocity.

It should be of great concern to the whole society that we are combatting inflation in this way, having, through deregulation, given up the tools to directly combat inflation at its source. The government and the RBA have little direct control over the level and profile of bank credit creation.

This point is so important that it warrants repeating. At present, our monetary policy settings work sharply in tension with bank money creation through lending – a process over which monetary authorities have surrendered direct control.

By switching to the New Zealand model of inflation targeting, via the setting of interest rates, the RBA does not and cannot address the direct source of national inflation.

In giving up controls over bank lending, the Australian government and the central bank have given up the means to control the principal cause of Australian inflation directly.

As John Law's financial innovations did in the eighteenth century, Australia's giant monetary experiment seems to be reshaping the economy and causing large and arbitrary transfers of wealth, in this case towards the housing and banking sectors and away from the rest of the economy. This dynamic has likely been building for more than 30 years, and the failure to recognise the possibility of this may be the biggest policy mistake of all.

Could it be that Australia's major economic institutions and financial 'wiring' are incompatible with the current bipartisan light-touch approach to economic and financial regulation? There is a strong case for a new approach featuring careful management of the financial system to ensure it supports economic growth and otherwise serves the public interest.

One specific failure in our regulatory architecture: commercial banks are largely regulated from a prudential perspective, but there is little regard for the impact of banks on productivity or economic growth. In our current siloed approach to financial regulation, no one owns the economy-wide considerations associated with achieving a desirable balance of productive and unproductive lending.

In Part I, I outlined an intuitive, nine-point orthodoxy about money, taxation and the financial system. Now, based on the trains of thought we have followed, I can briefly state an alternative and correct orthodoxy:

- Bank money – in the form of contractual, ledger-based IOUs – is by far the dominant form of money in the economy today. It is 'official' only indirectly, and its quality depends on the creditworthiness of the bank that holds it. Ledger-based money is not tradable, and it only 'moves' through the economy in a metaphorical sense. Putting aside notes and coins, 'the Australian dollar' (like 'the Pound' and 'the US dollar') exists only in the abstract.
- Taxation at the national level is a means to take liquidity from the economy, mostly by erasing ledger-based bank-money balances. Governments do not and cannot hold

money outside the banking system (aside from notes and coins). When governments spend, they spend money into existence at that time.

- Due to a self-imposed fiscal rule, the money created through government spending is exactly offset by money destruction through taxation and borrowing. Governments that follow that rule do not increase the money supply, even when running deficits.
- Banks do not turn deposits into loans. The money in a loan account is created anew, at the time of the loan and at no direct cost to the bank. (The ability to do this distinguishes banks from goldsmiths.) Banks do not intermediate between depositors and borrowers. Banks receive profits that are very much out of step with the modest functions they perform and the modest risks they manage.
- Banking's two-tier nature is one of its defining features. Reserves are on the higher tier, above ordinary bank deposits. Banks cannot fail due to a shortage of deposits, but they can fail due to a shortage of reserves, which serve as systemic media for settling inter-bank payments. Fractional reserve banking is a misnomer based on a misunderstanding of how banking works.
- Central banks do not and cannot use reserves to control the money supply. Central bank and commercial bank balance sheets are decoupled. In ordinary circumstances, the quantum of reserves is not a binding constraint on money creation. The terms 'base money' and 'high-powered money', when applied to reserves, are misleading because,

among other things, reserves are not money. They can only be held by banks, and they are not part of the purchasing economy.

- Reserves held on deposit by private banks with the central bank are not truly liabilities of the central bank. The reserves are created with no direct cost, and they do not give rise to any exchange obligations for the central bank, such as the obligation to exchange reserve balances for gold. They are better thought of as clearing and settlement units. Current accounting of reserves reflects a bygone era.
- Growth in the money supply (and, in principle, changes in money velocity) determines the level of inflation. As money velocity in Australia has fallen sharply over recent decades, it is not contributing to inflation. Bank money creation is the main cause of money supply growth, and hence it is the main cause of inflation in the economy. Other factors – such as aggregate demand, systemic cost increases and wage demands – merely affect the composition of inflation, not the level.
- Even though inflation is caused primarily by bank lending, the Australian government and the central bank have, under the banner of financial deregulation, given up controls over such lending. Hence, instead of tackling inflation at its direct source, the government and the RBA combat inflation through a crude, indirect, economy-wide approach. As a result, interest rates are higher than they would otherwise be, as are taxes and the exchange rate, potentially imposing a significant burden on non-banking and non-housing sectors such as manufacturing.

A tenth point to add to the list:

- Most new money in the economy is created through bank lending; and in Australia, the bulk of bank lending is for residential property. In other words, bank-financed purchases of residential property are the main source of new money in the economy. The overall level of property prices is not independent of this process.

If Australia has botched its monetary institutional arrangements and policy settings, how could this situation best be unwound?

The challenge will be to balance two burning imperatives: ameliorating the process of unfettered money creation distorting the economy and gradually stifling the non-bank economy; and avoiding the risk of widescale property wealth destruction and the substantial negative consequences that would cause.

Meeting that challenge will require an economic policy reset.

But such a reset is achievable. The federal government could gradually reinstate some reasonable quantitative and qualitative limits on bank lending, especially for speculative and unproductive loans and those that inflate asset markets. A restored legislative power to influence the profile of bank lending could be used to carefully slow the currency-collateral-currency cycle and to make room for more beneficial forms of lending and money creation.

Importantly, reasonable limits on bank money creation would enable the government and the central bank to control inflation at its source rather than in a blunt and crude way at the economy-wide level.

Such limits would also create space for more beneficial lending and more beneficial money creation.

To make use of that headroom, the government could take steps to recover some public control over currency issuance and to directly increase productive lending, such as by establishing a new, publicly owned, industry development bank, possibly modelled on the UK's publicly owned British Business Bank or the Development Bank of Wales.

The emergence of digital currencies provides a further means for the government to restore some public control over our currency in a way that complements rather than depends upon bank money creation.

Specifically, the government could issue a new, secure, government-backed digital currency. Controlled by the national parliament, issuance of the new currency would further help achieve a better balance of money creation across the economy, and it would enable new forms of banking, such as credit-risk-free deposit accounts.

These steps would take some of the inflation reduction burden from the non-banking parts of the economy and allow the profile of lending to be improved, with greater lending for productive purposes – including lending to innovative small and medium-sized businesses and for publicly beneficial projects such as housing construction, clean energy and digital infrastructure. Those types of lending are routes to genuine prosperity.[1]

In addition, there is scope to rethink how we invest in public benefit projects.

As noted, fiscal policy should be thought of as operating within an inflation constraint, rather than a budget constraint. And within our inflation constraint, project evaluation criteria should be about the overall economic, social and environmental benefits, not about beating an artificial budget constraint or an imaginary cost of capital hurdle.

An antidote to the downward spiral of 'austerity', more astute use of our national fiscal capacity is a route towards productive and pro-social investment on a vastly enhanced scale.

1 In general, by placing constraints on bank lending from time to time to curtail private bank money creation, there would be greater scope for beneficial net money creation – including through government spending – elsewhere in the economy.

Finally, and in parallel to these systemic initiatives, we need to think about a reformed and refreshed set of national economic institutions that focus on the public interest, rather than narrow sectoral ones. And, ultimately, we need to improve our collective understanding of how money works, so we can avoid stepping once more into a giant monetary policy trap.

Postscript

Australia's final step in bank deregulation took place just last year

Until recently, Section 36 of the *Banking Act 1959* contained a residual and somewhat ambiguous power for the RBA to direct the lending activities of banks:

> Where the Reserve Bank is satisfied that it is necessary or expedient to do so in the public interest, the Reserve Bank may determine the policy in relation to advances to be followed by ADIs [Authorised Deposit-taking Institutions, that is, banks].

The 2022–23 review of the RBA recommended the removal of that power (which had not been used since deregulation) on the grounds that its purpose was unclear and it was not necessary for the fulfilment of the RBA's 'core mandate' vis-à-vis the prudential mandate of the Australian Prudential Regulation Authority (APRA).[1]

Though APRA assumed some powers relating to bank lending, that power was only available 'for purposes of financial safety and financial stability' and not for money supply control or for other public policy goals such as increasing the economic benefits of bank lending. The Australian government accepted the review recommendation, and the repeal of the RBA's bank lending power in Section 36 of the *Banking Act 1959* took effect in early 2025.

1 RBA Review Panel (2023).

Appendix: Figures

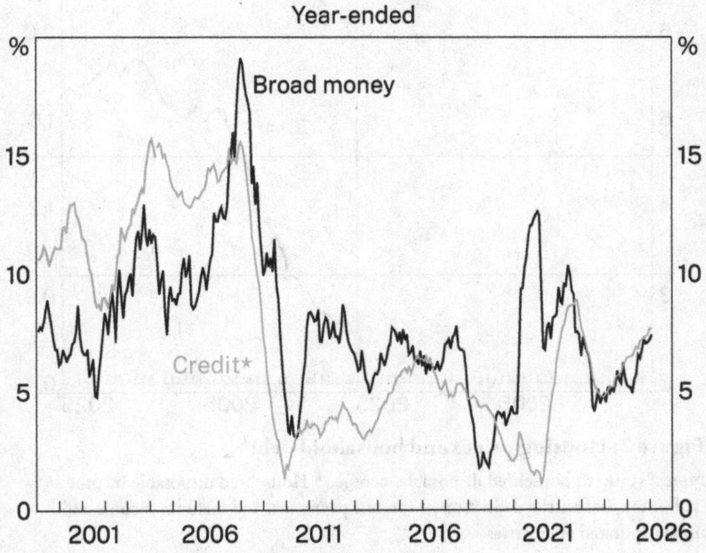

Figure 1: Credit and broad money growth

Notes: * Excluding financial business post May 2004. Seasonally adjusted and break-adjusted; including securitisation.

Sources: RBA (2026), p.11. Compiled from ABS, APRA and RBA data.

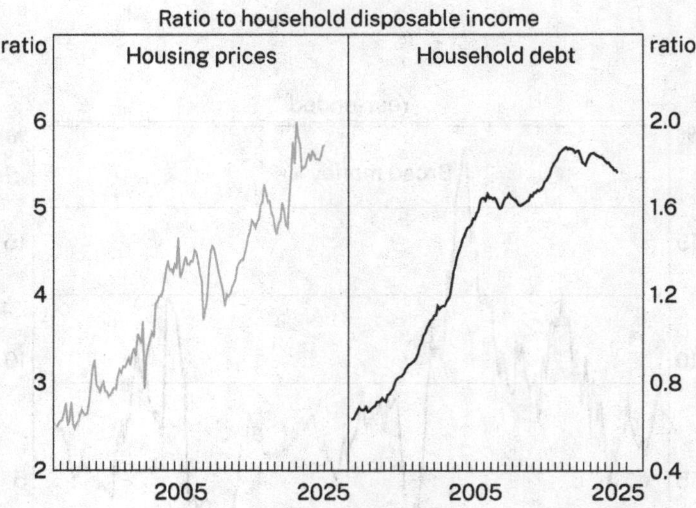

Figure 2: Housing prices and household debt*

Notes: Ratio to household disposable income. * Household disposable income is after tax, before the deduction of interest payments, and includes income and unincorporated enterprises.

Sources: RBA (2026), p.7. Compiled from ABS, Cotality and RBA data.

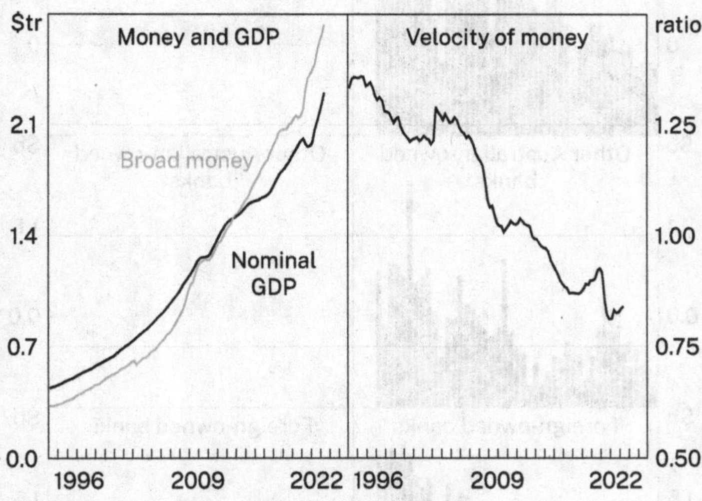

Figure 3: Quantity theory of money

Sources: RBA (n.d.). Compiled from ABS, APRA and RBA data.

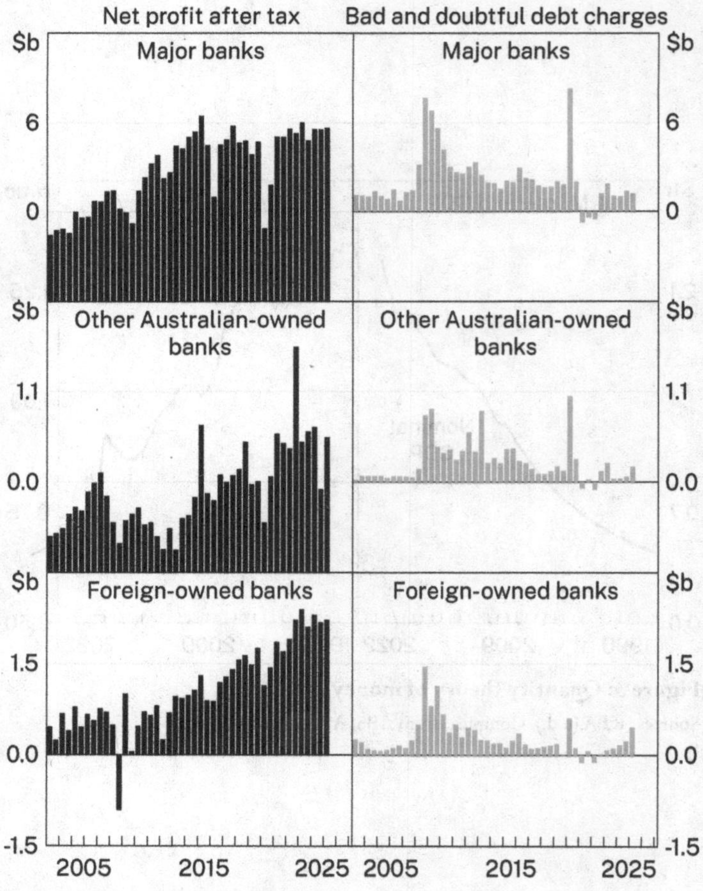

Figure 4: Australian bank profits

Sources: RBA (2026), p.31. Compiled from APRA and RBA data.

References

Black, Jes (2021) 'Chester A. Phillips and the forgotten history of bank credit', PhD thesis, Universitat de Barcelona.

Bodin, Jean (1568) *Réponse de J. Bodin aux paradoxes de M. de Malestroit*, Paris: Martin le Jeune.

Bradley, Chris, Ben Stretch, Jules Carrigan and Wesley Walden (2025) 'Five big tests for Australia's productivity agenda', McKinsey Australia and New Zealand.

Campbell Committee of Inquiry (1981) *Australian Financial System: Final Report of the Committee of Inquiry*, Canberra: Australian Government Publishing Service. treasury.gov.au/publication/p1981-afs.

Cantillon, Richard (1755) *Essai sur la Nature du Commerce en Général* (*Essay on the Nature of Trade in General*), written between 1730 and 1734 and published posthumously in 1755.

Copernicus, Nicolaus (1526) *Monetae cudendae ratio* (a report written at the request of King Sigismund I of Poland).

Federal Reserve Bank of St Louis (2018) 'How does the federal reserve control the supply of money?' www.stlouisfed.org/on-the-economy/2018/july/federal-reserve-control-supply-money (accessed August 2025).

Friedman, Milton (1987) 'Monetarism', in John Eatwell, Murray Milgate and Peter Newman, eds, *The New Palgrave: A Dictionary of Economics*, London: Macmillan.

Friedman, Milton (1960) *A Program for Monetary Stability*, New York: Fordham University Press.

Galbraith, John Kenneth (2017) *Money: Whence It Came, Where It Went*, Princeton: Princeton University Press. doi.org/10.23943/princeton/9780691171661.001.0001.

Gollan, Robin (1968) *The Commonwealth Bank of Australia: Origins and early history*, Canbera: Australian National University Press.

Hayek, Friedrich (1931) *Prices and Production*, London: George Routledge and Sons Ltd. (published in German as *Preise und Produktion*).

Hume, David (1752) *Political Discourses* (part II of *Essays, Moral, Political, and Literary* within *Essays and Treatises on Several Subjects*, vol. 1).

Johnston, R.A. (May 1985) 'Monetary policy: The changing environment', T.A. Coghlan Memorial Lecture, University of New South Wales.

Kells, Stuart (2024a) *Alice: Biggest Untold Story in the History of Money*, Melbourne: Melbourne University Publishing.

Kells, Stuart (2024b) 'Money may make the world go round, but what is it exactly?', *Pursuit*, University of Melbourne.

Keynes, John Maynard (1930) *A Treatise on Money*, London: Macmillan & Co.

Kohler, Alan (2019) *It's Your Money: How Banking Went Rogue, Where it is Now and How to Protect and Grow Your Money*, Melbourne: Black Inc.

Kohler, Alan (2023) 'The great divide: Australia's housing mess and how to fix it', *Quarterly Essay* 92.

Kuznets, Simon (1951) 'National income and industrial structure', Proceedings of the International Statistical Conferences, 1947, vol. 5, 205–39. As reprinted in S. Kuznets (1954) *Economic Change*, London: William Heinemann.

Kuznets, Simon (1941) *National Income and Its Composition, 1919–1938*, New York: National Bureau of Economic Research.

Law, John (c. 1704) 'Essay on a land bank'.

Law, John (1705) 'Money and trade considered'.

Lim, Guay (2025) Retirement speech, unpublished, Melbourne Institute, 28 August 2025.

Loyd, Samuel Jones (Lord Overstone) (1858) *The Evidence Given by Lord Overstone before the Select Committee of the House of Commons of 1857 on Bank Acts, with Additions*, London: Longman, Brown.

McLeay, Michael, Amar Radia and Ryland Thomas (2014) 'Money creation in the modern economy', *Bank of England Quarterly Bulletin*, Q1.

Merrett, David (2000) 'Paying for it all', in Patrick Troy, ed., *A History of European Housing in Australia*, Melbourne: Cambridge University Press.

Mill, John Stuart (1844) 'Review of books by Thomas Tooke and R. Torrens', *Westminster Review*, June.

NAB (30 October 2025) 'NAB's $60 billion ambition to help tackle the housing crisis', *NAB News*, news.nab.com.au/tag/housing-property/nab-s--60-billion-ambition-to-help-tackle-the-housing-crisis-.

Navarro, Martín de Azpilcueta Navarro (1556) *Comentario resolutorio de usuras*, Salamanque.

Norman, George Warde (1841) *Letter to Charles Wood, esq., M.P., on Money, and the Means of Economizing the Use of it*, London: P. Richardson.

O'Brien, D. P. (2007) *The Development of Monetary Economics: A Modern Perspective on Monetary Controversies*, Cheltenham: Edward Elgar. doi.org/10.4337/9781782542322.

Pigou, A.C. (1949) *The Veil of Money*, London: Macmillan & Co.

RBA Review Panel (March 2023) *Review of the Reserve Bank of Australia: An RBA Fit for the Future*, Final report, Australian Government, rbareview.gov.au/final-report.

Reserve Bank of Australia (October 2017) 'Box B: Households' investment property exposures: Insights from tax data', in *Financial Stability Review October 2017*, www.rba.gov.au/publications/fsr/2017/oct/box-b.html.

Reserve Bank of Australia (2025) 'Government bond purchases', RBA, www.rba.gov.au/mkt-operations/government-bond-purchases.html (accessed August 2025).

Reserve Bank of Australia (May 2026) 'The Australian economy and financial markets: Chart pack', RBA, www.rba.gov.au/chart-pack/.

Reserve Bank of Australia (n.d.) 'Review of the Bond Purchase Program', www.rba.gov.au/monetary-policy/reviews/bond-purchase-program/index.html (accessed August 2025).

Robertson, Dennis (1922) *Money*, New York: Harcourt, Brace.

Standing Committee on Economics (2026) 'Review of the Reserve Bank of Australia Annual Report 2025', Parliament of Australia. parlinfo.aph.gov.au/parlInfo/search/display/display.w3p;query=Id%3A%22committees%2Fcommrep%2F29126%2F0001%22;rec=0.

Tobin, James (1974) in Robert Gordon, *Milton Friedman's Monetary Framework: A debate with his critics*, Chicago: University of Chicago Press.

Torrens, Robert (1812): *An Essay on Money and Paper Currency*, London: Printed for J. Johnson and Co.

Wen, Yi (2015) 'The making of an economic superpower: Unlocking China's secret of rapid industrialization', Working Paper 2015-006B, June 2015, Federal Reserve Bank of St Louis Research Division, p.109. doi.org/10.20955/wp.2015.006.

Werner, Richard A. (2014) 'Can banks individually create money out of nothing? — The theories and the empirical evidence', *International Review of Financial Analysis*, 36: 1–19. doi.org/10.1016/j.irfa.2014.07.015.

Withers, Hartley (1915) 'Lombard street to-day', in Walter Bagehot, *Lombard Street*, London: John Murray, pp.vii-xix.

www.ingramcontent.com/pod-product-compliance
Lightning Source LLC
Chambersburg PA
CBHW021608130726
48054CB00040B/260

* 9 7 8 1 7 6 0 4 6 7 4 2 5 *